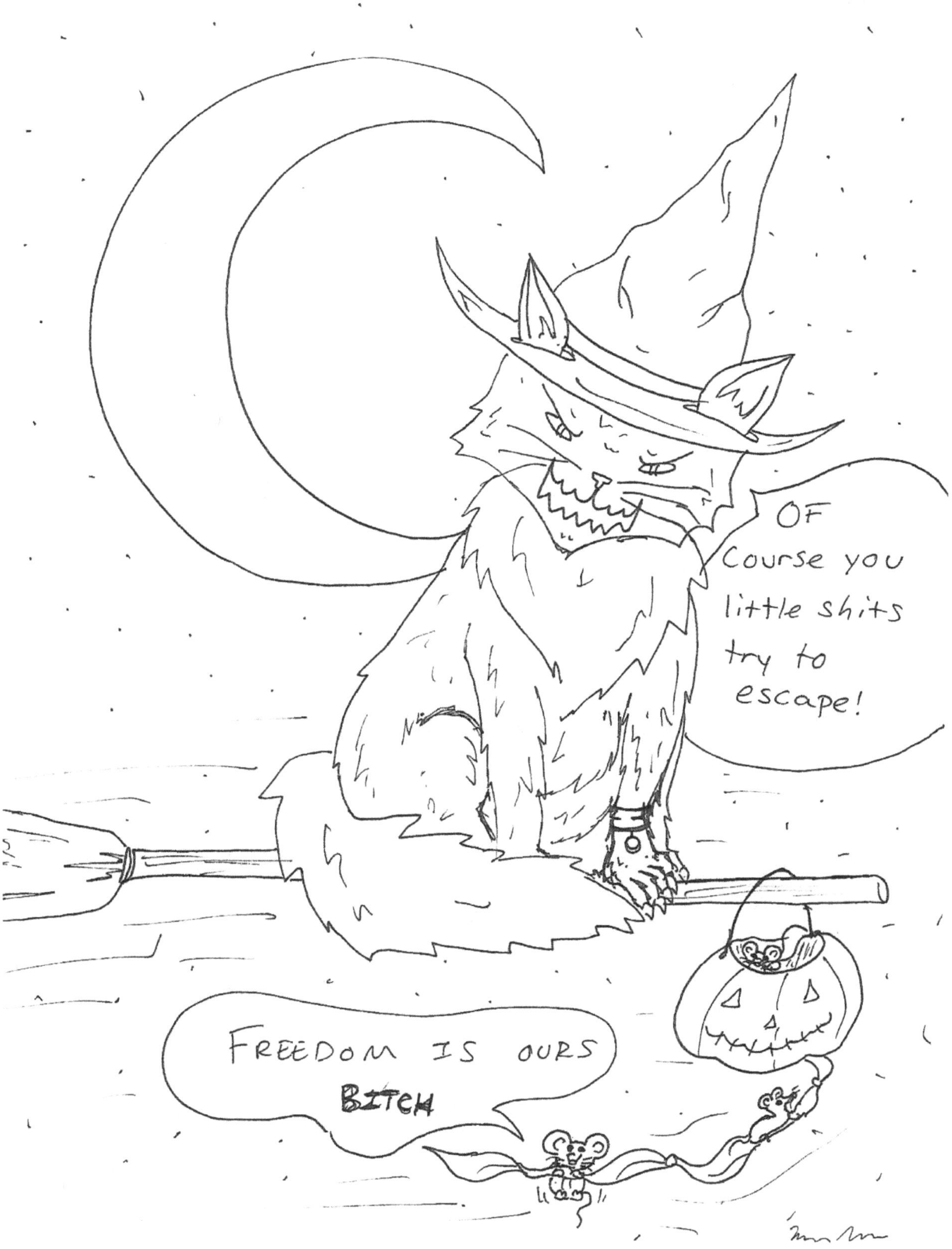

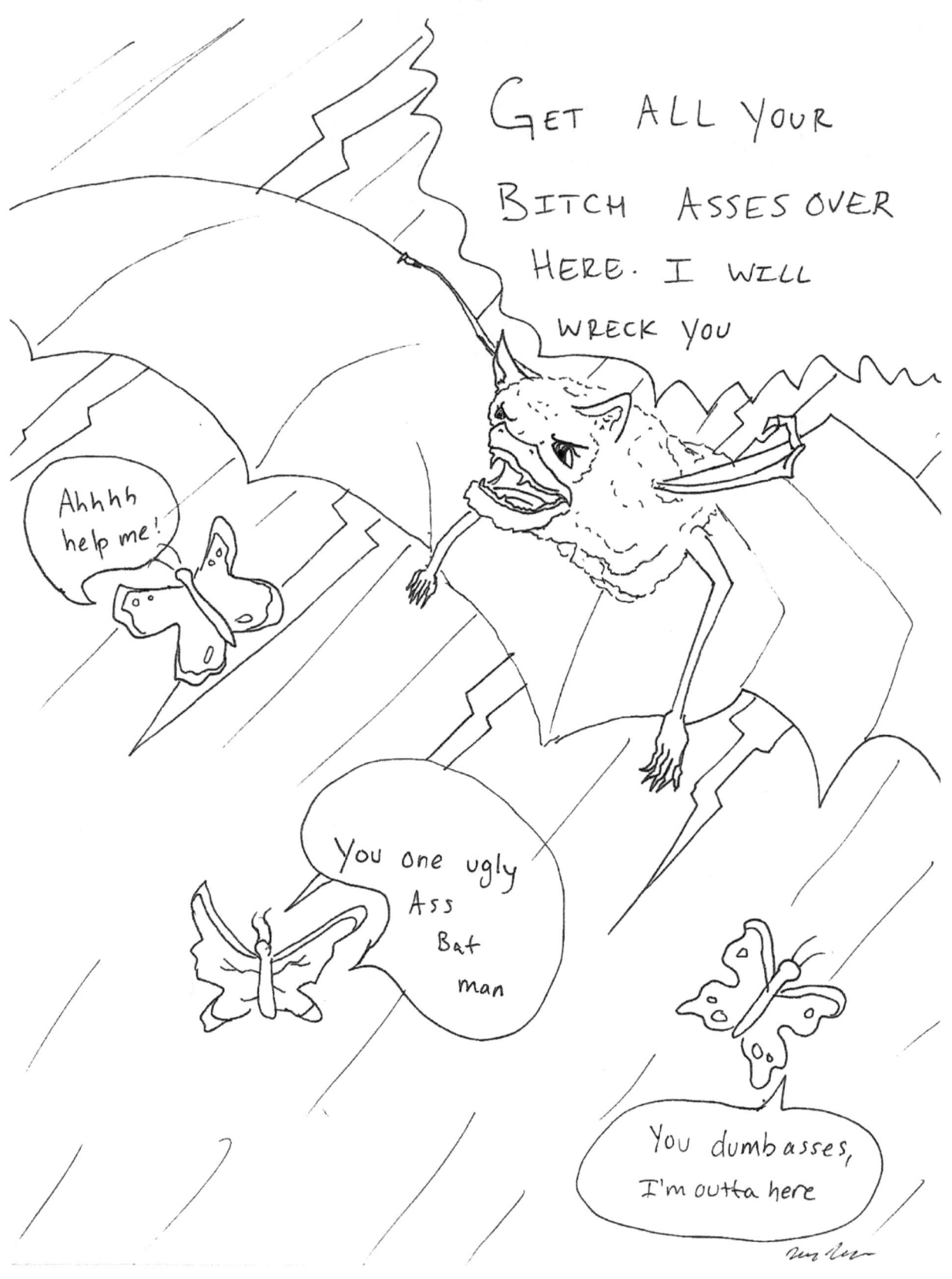

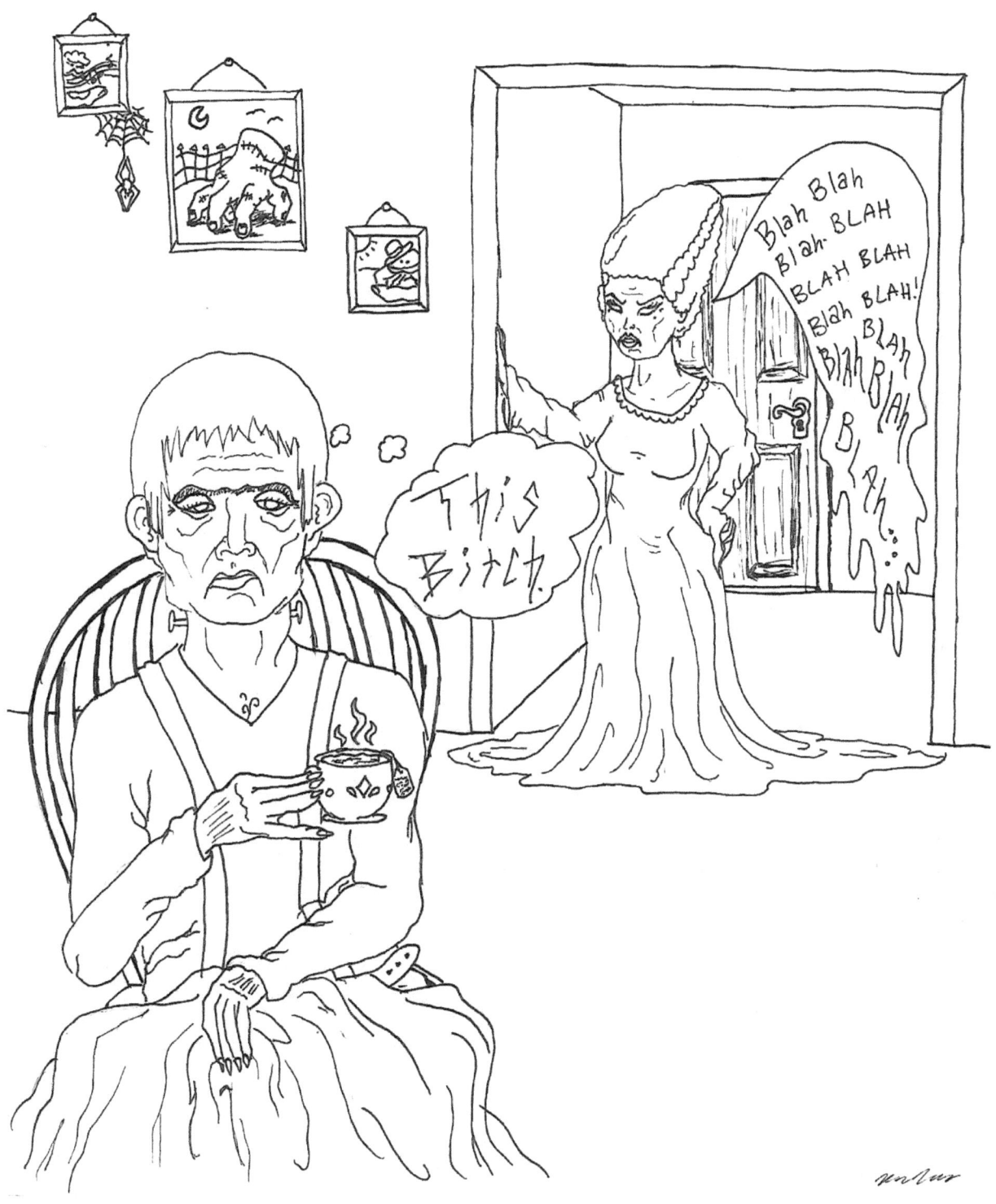

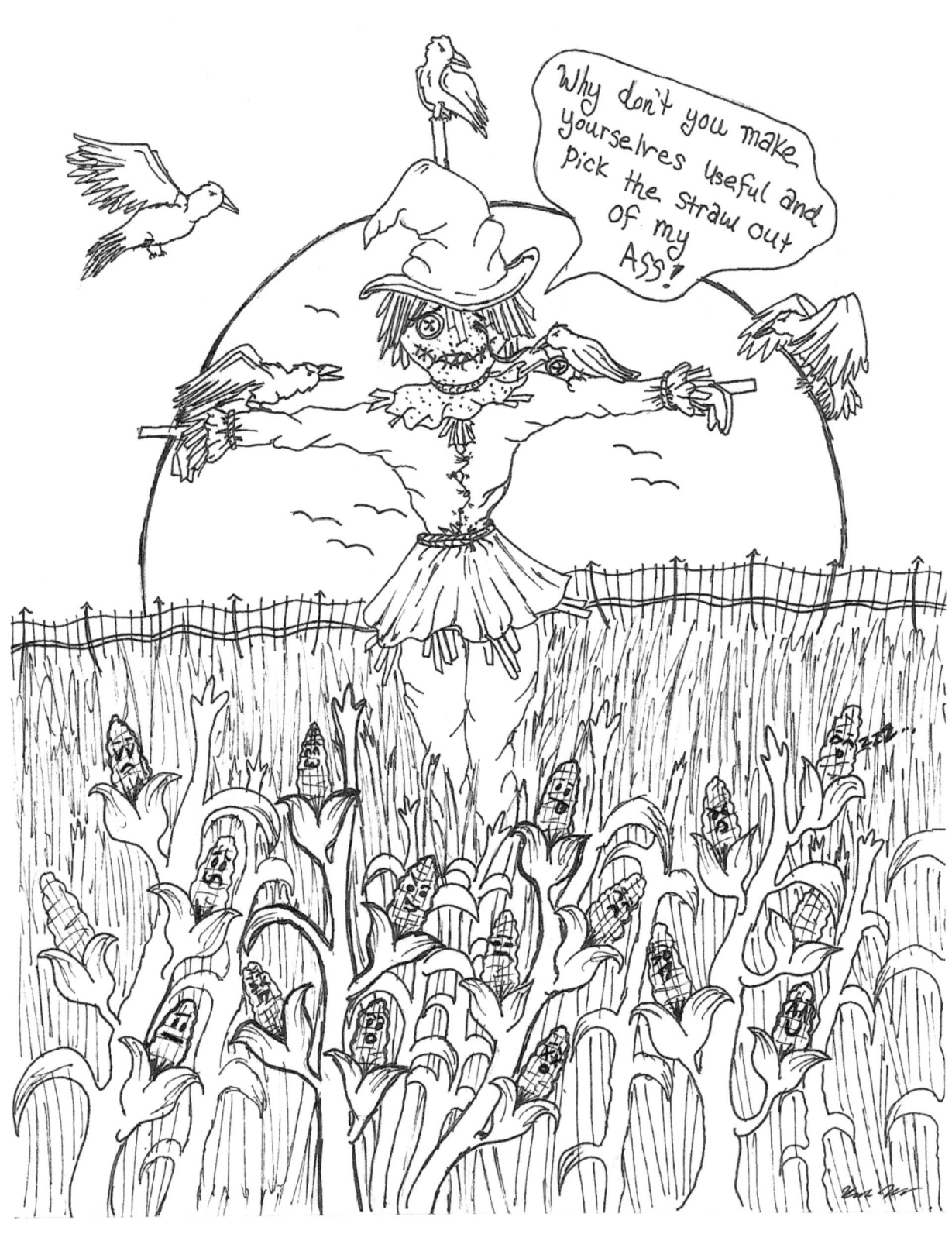

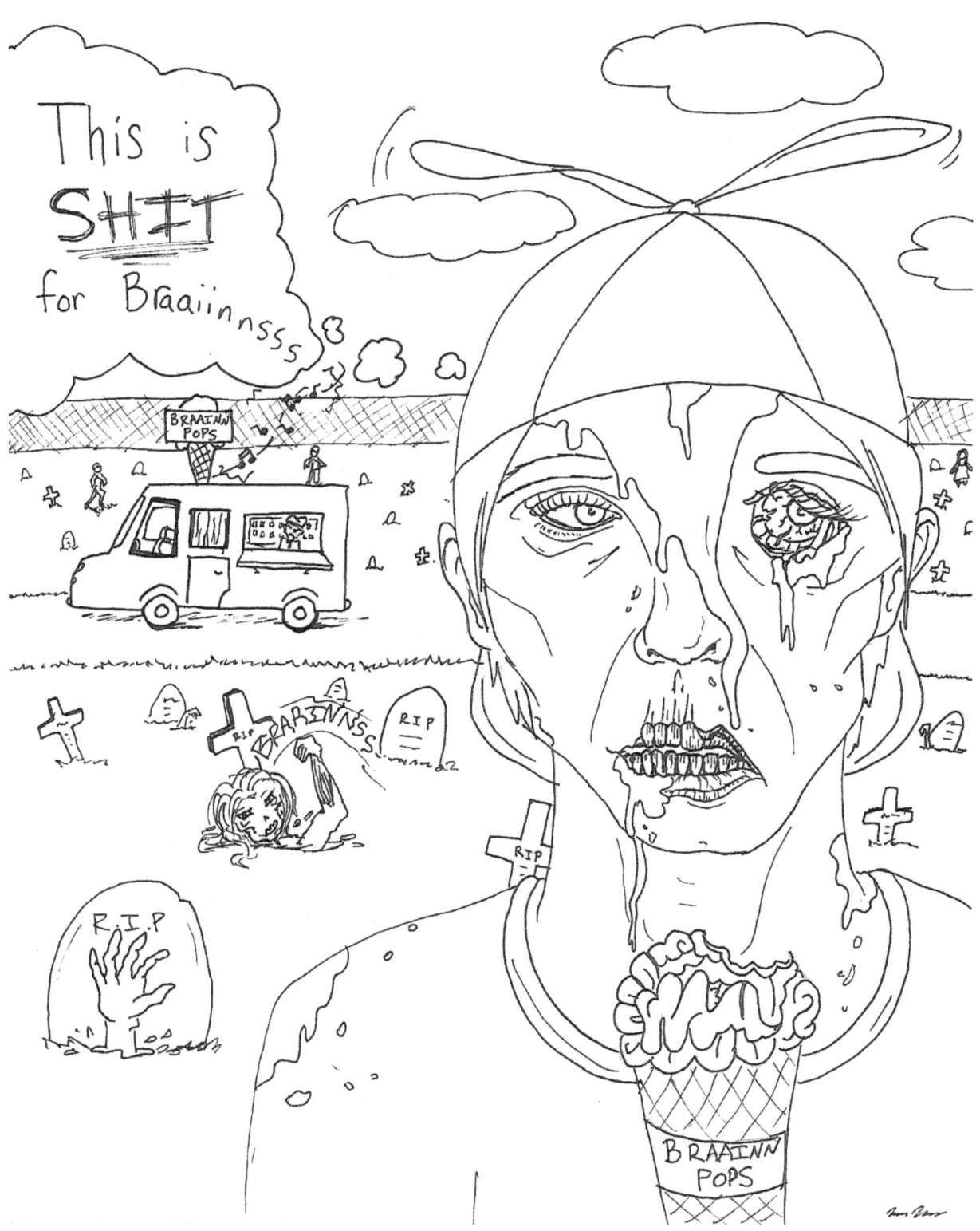

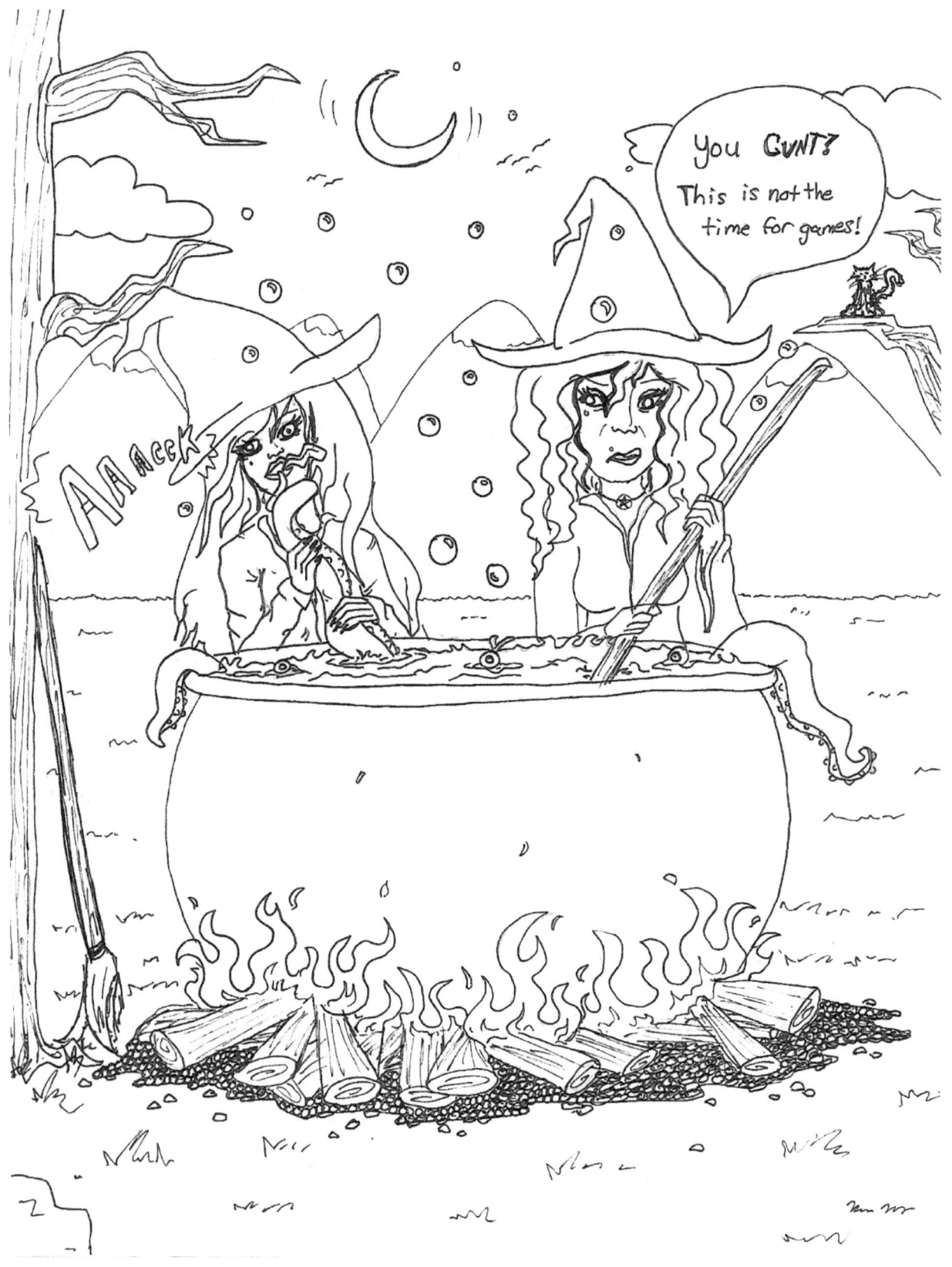

Listen UP Mothafucker! There's ONE WAY OUT... ONLY ONE; If you MAKE it that Far That is.

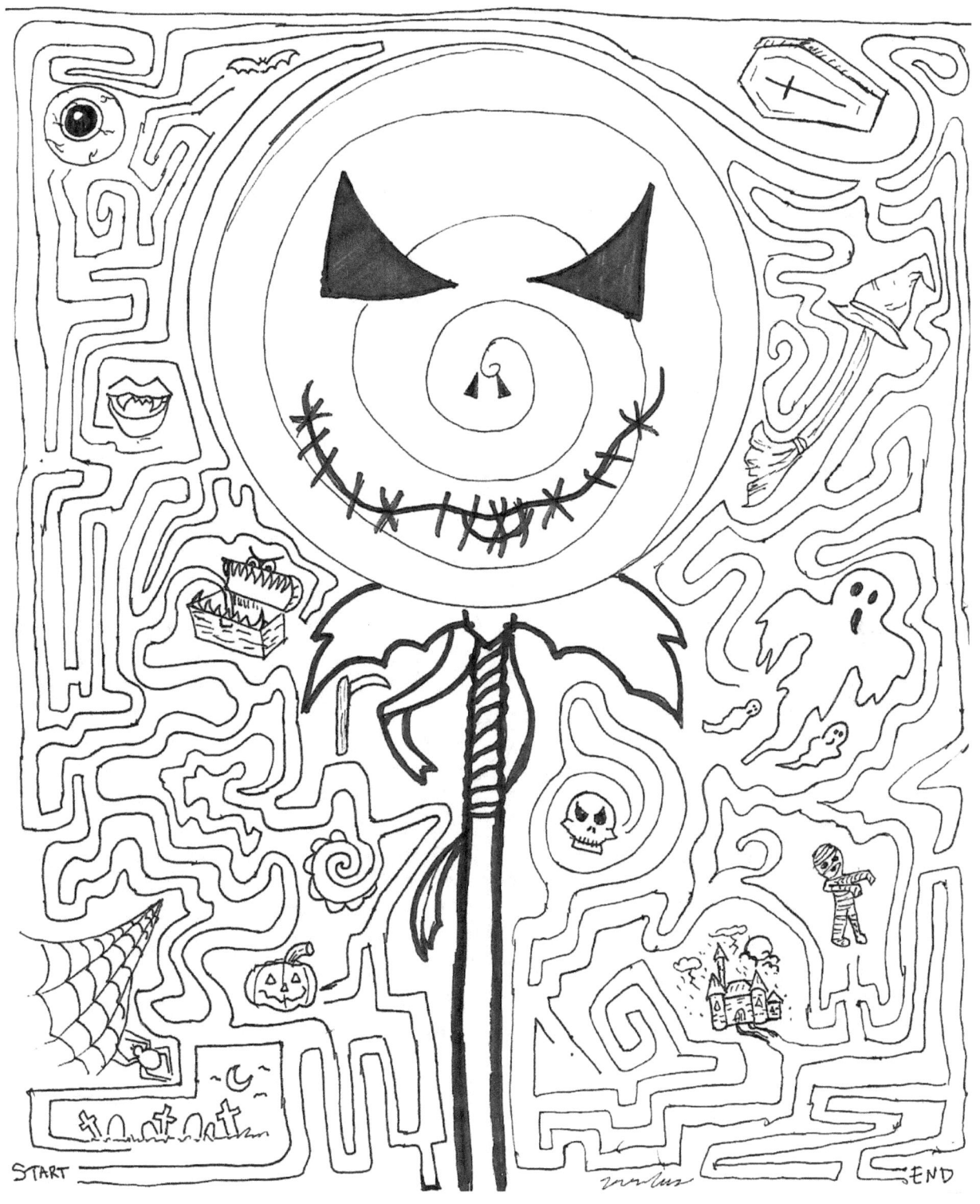

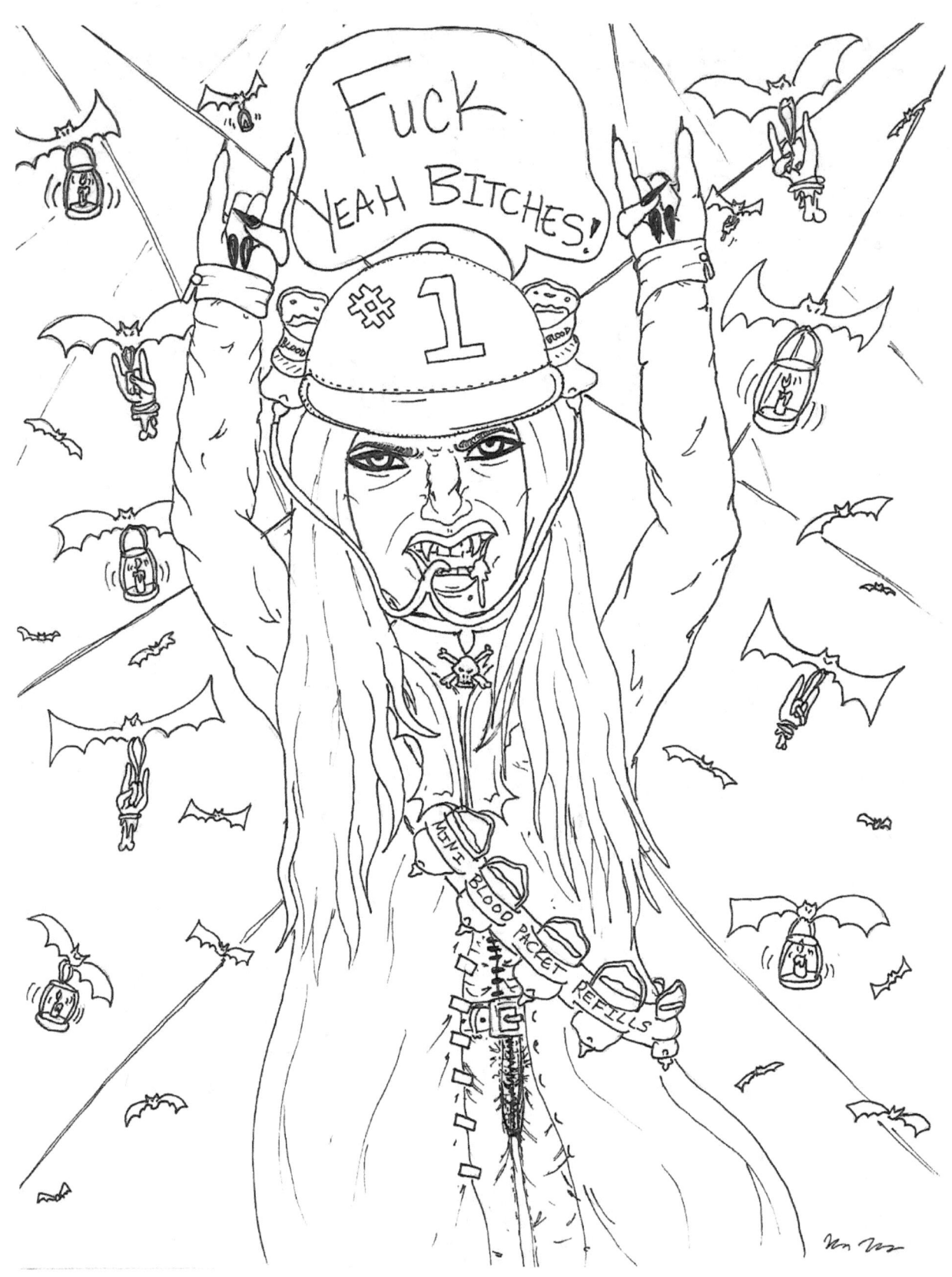

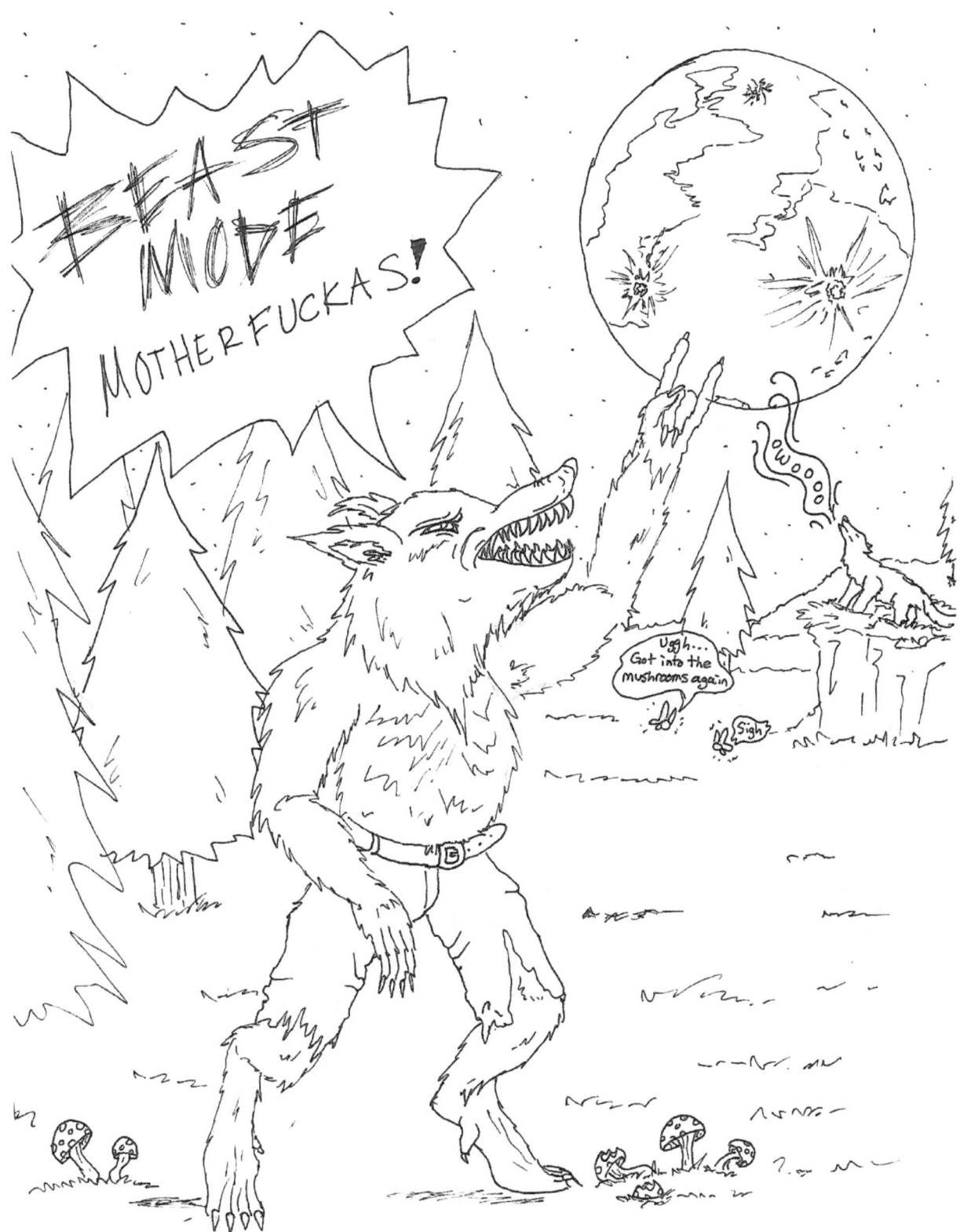

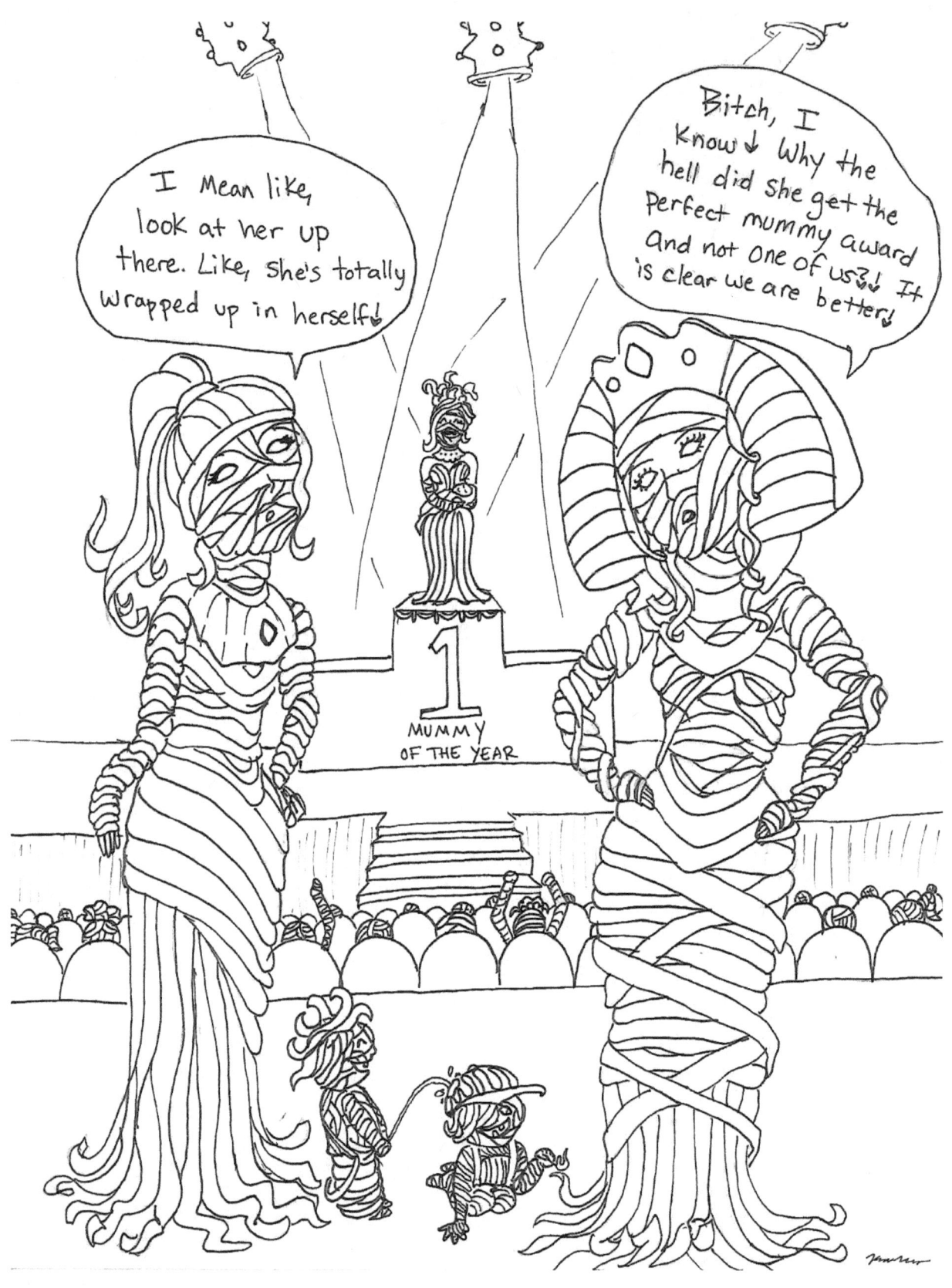

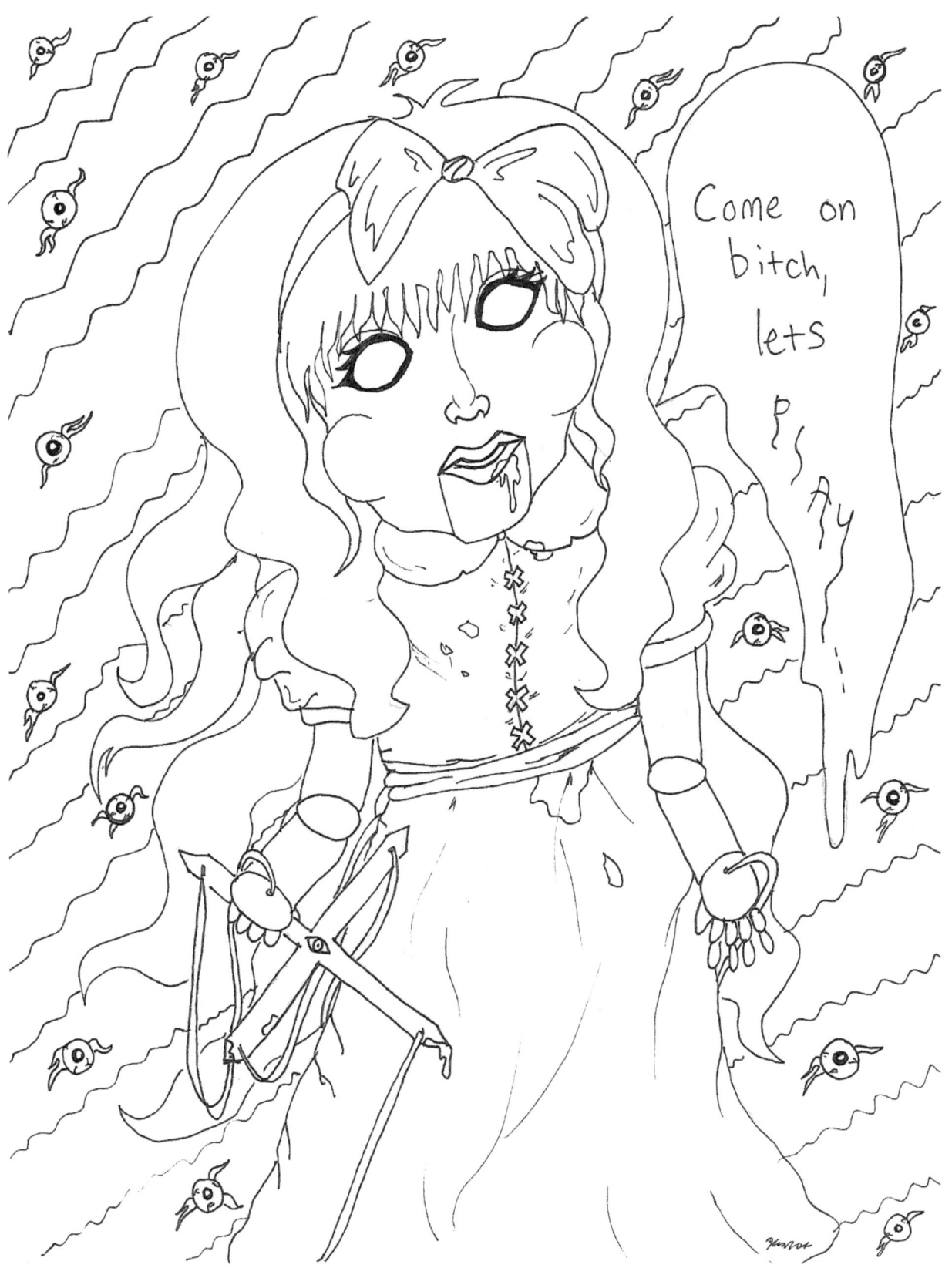

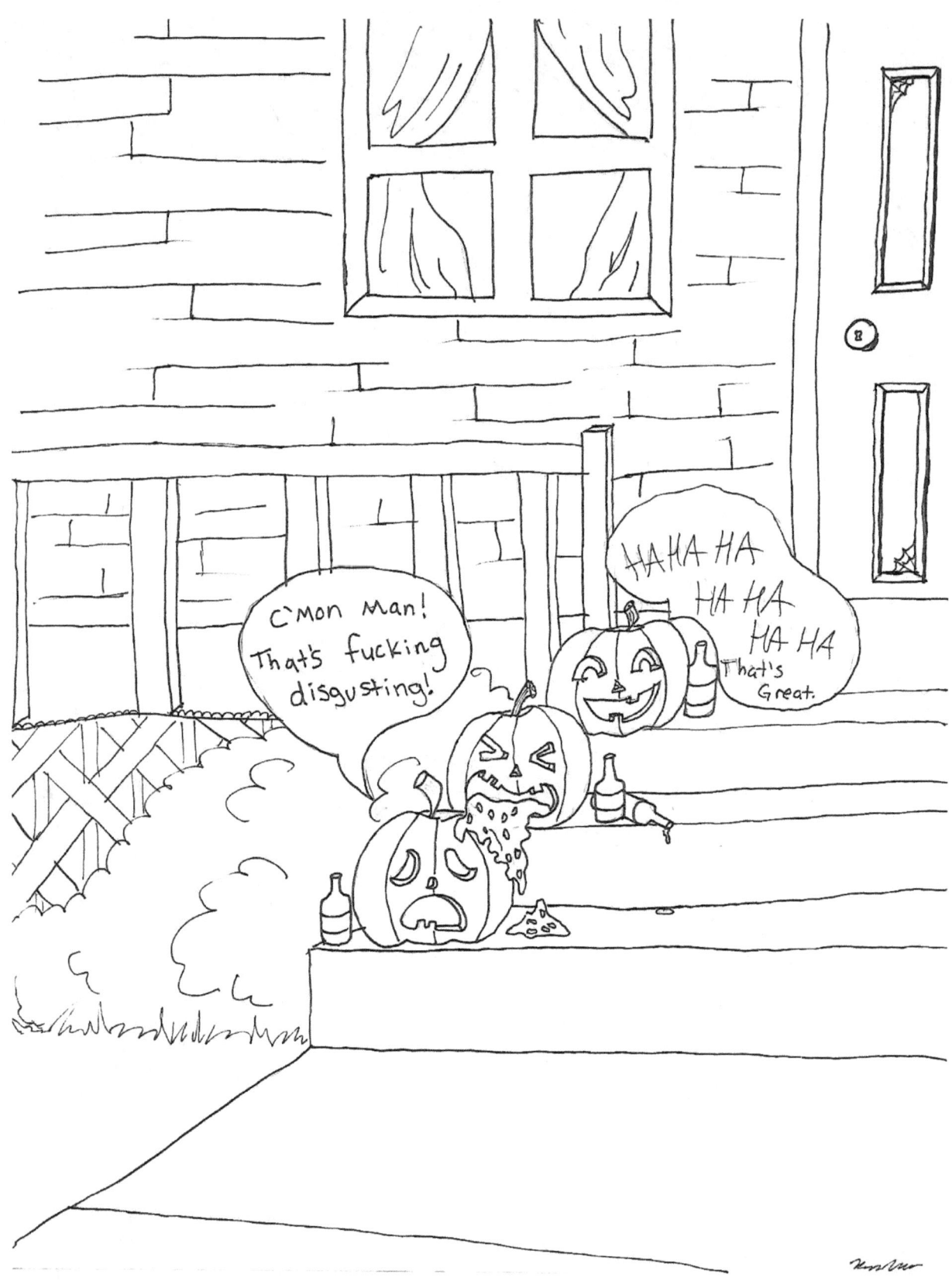

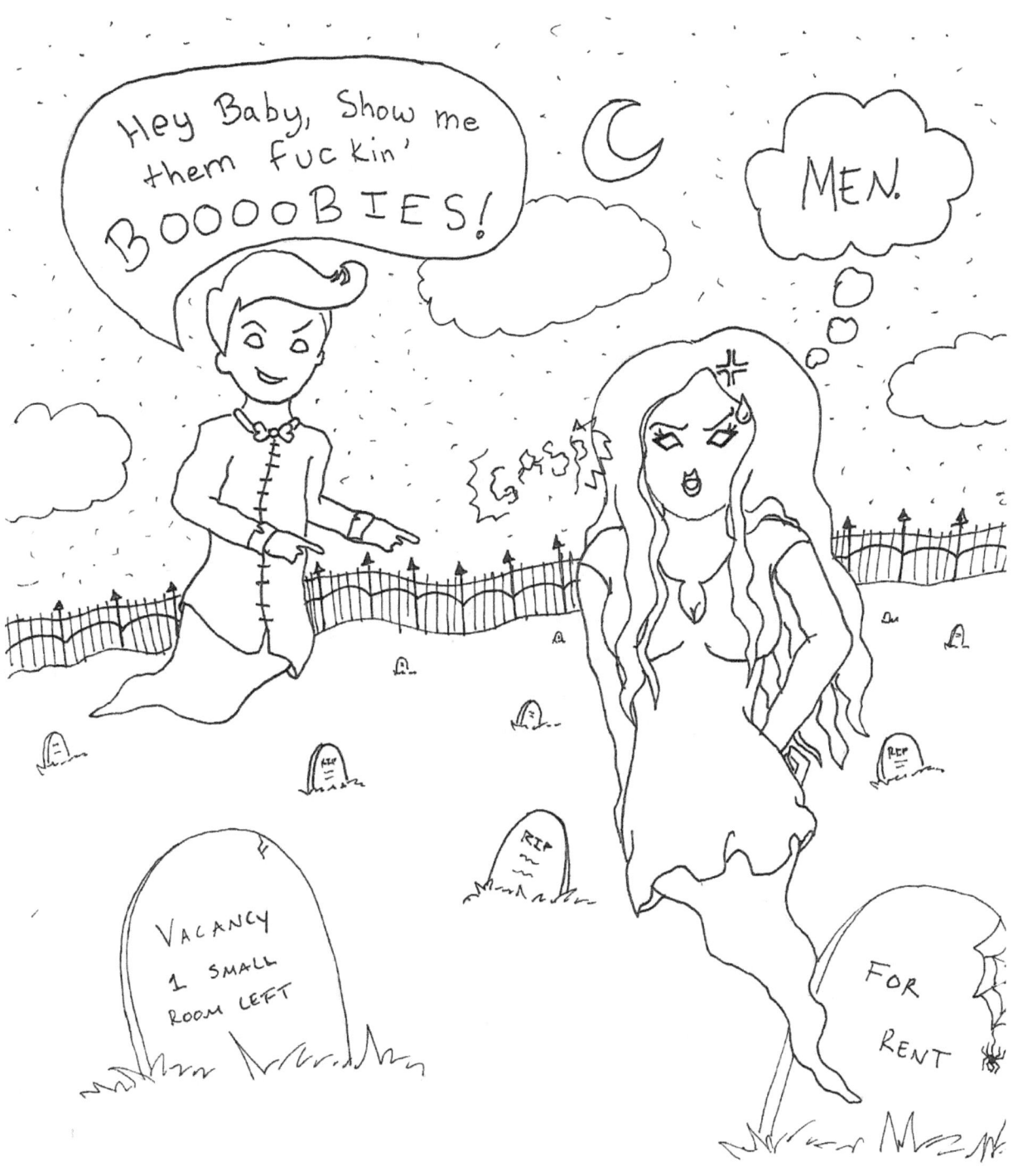

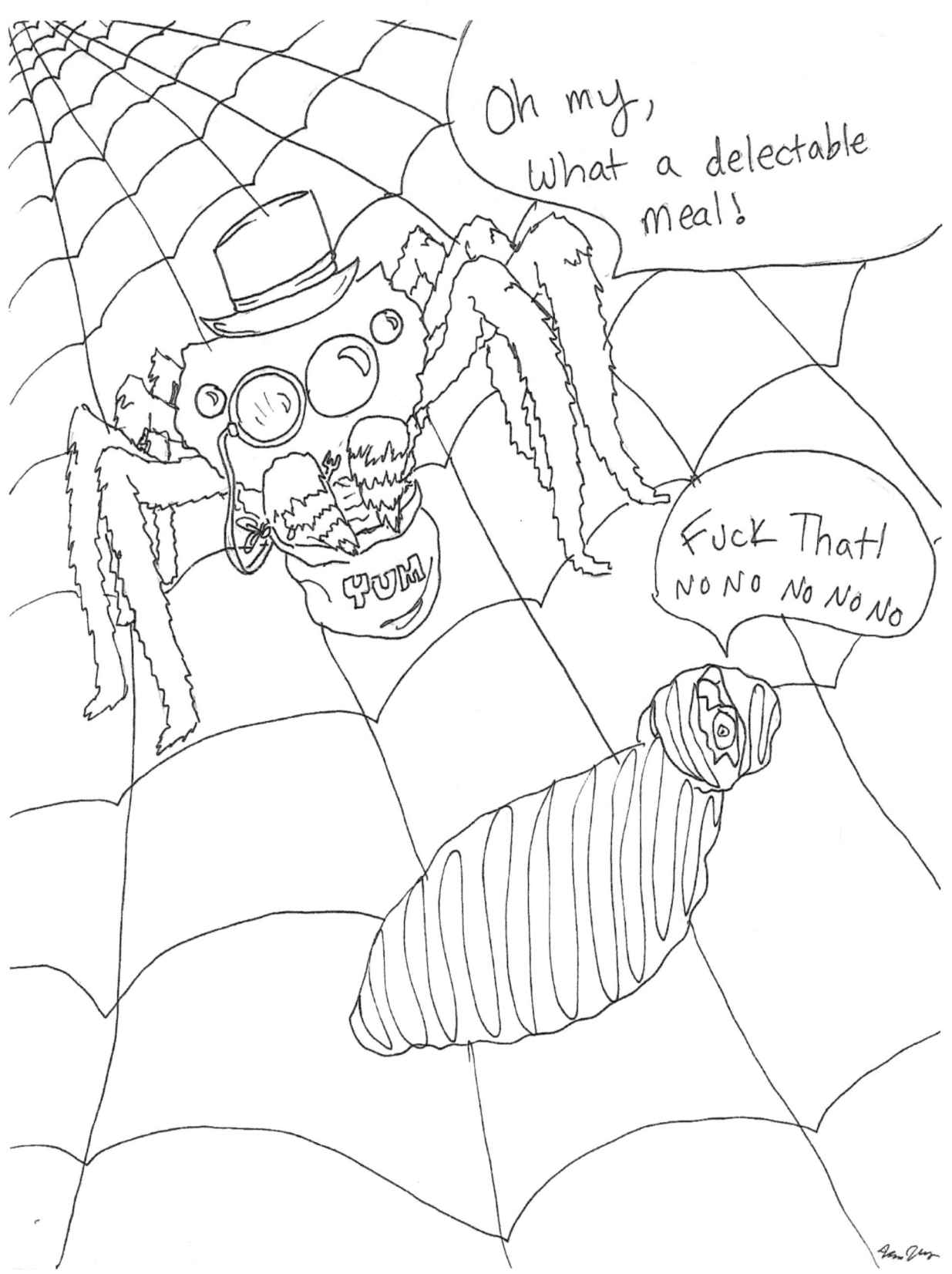

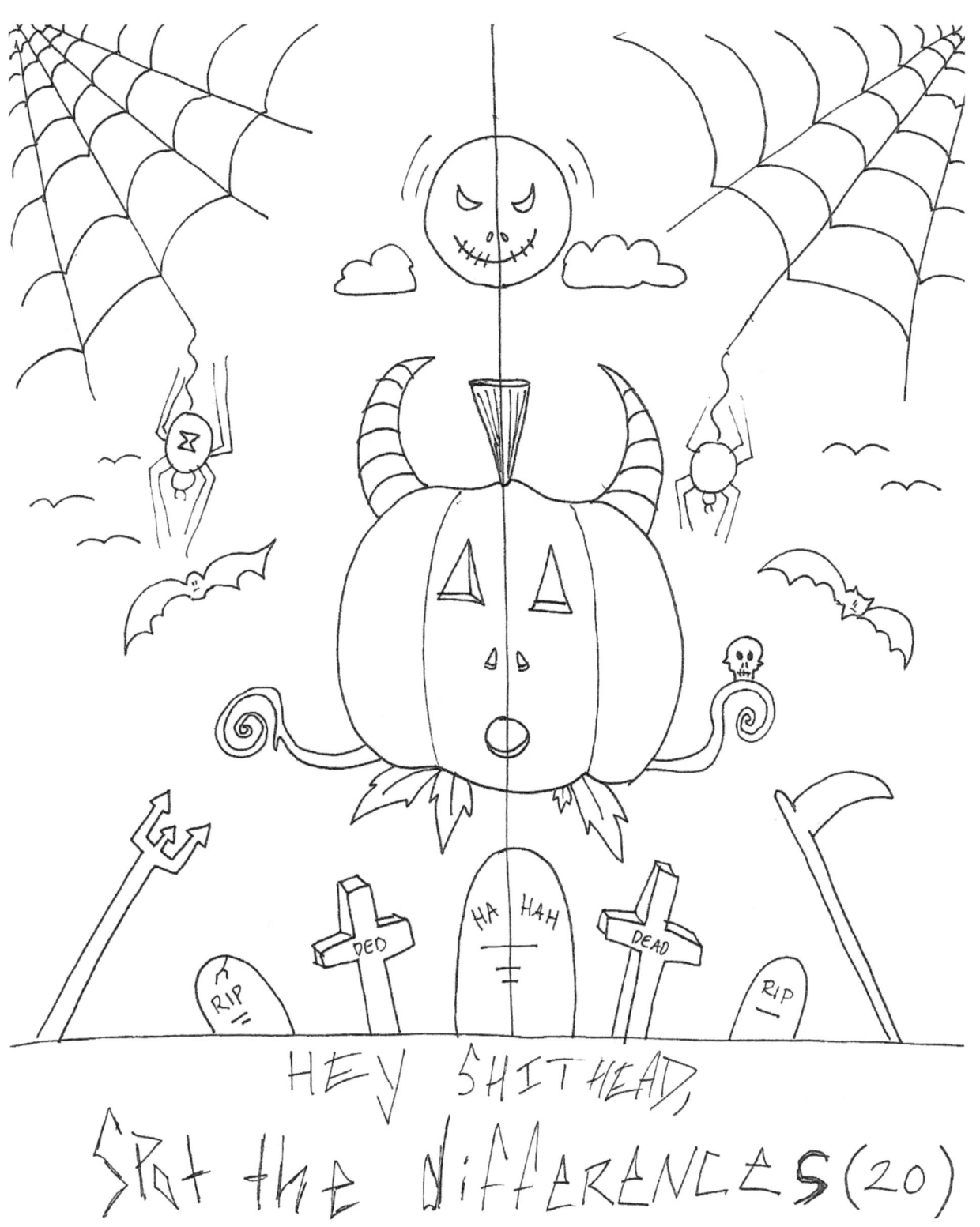

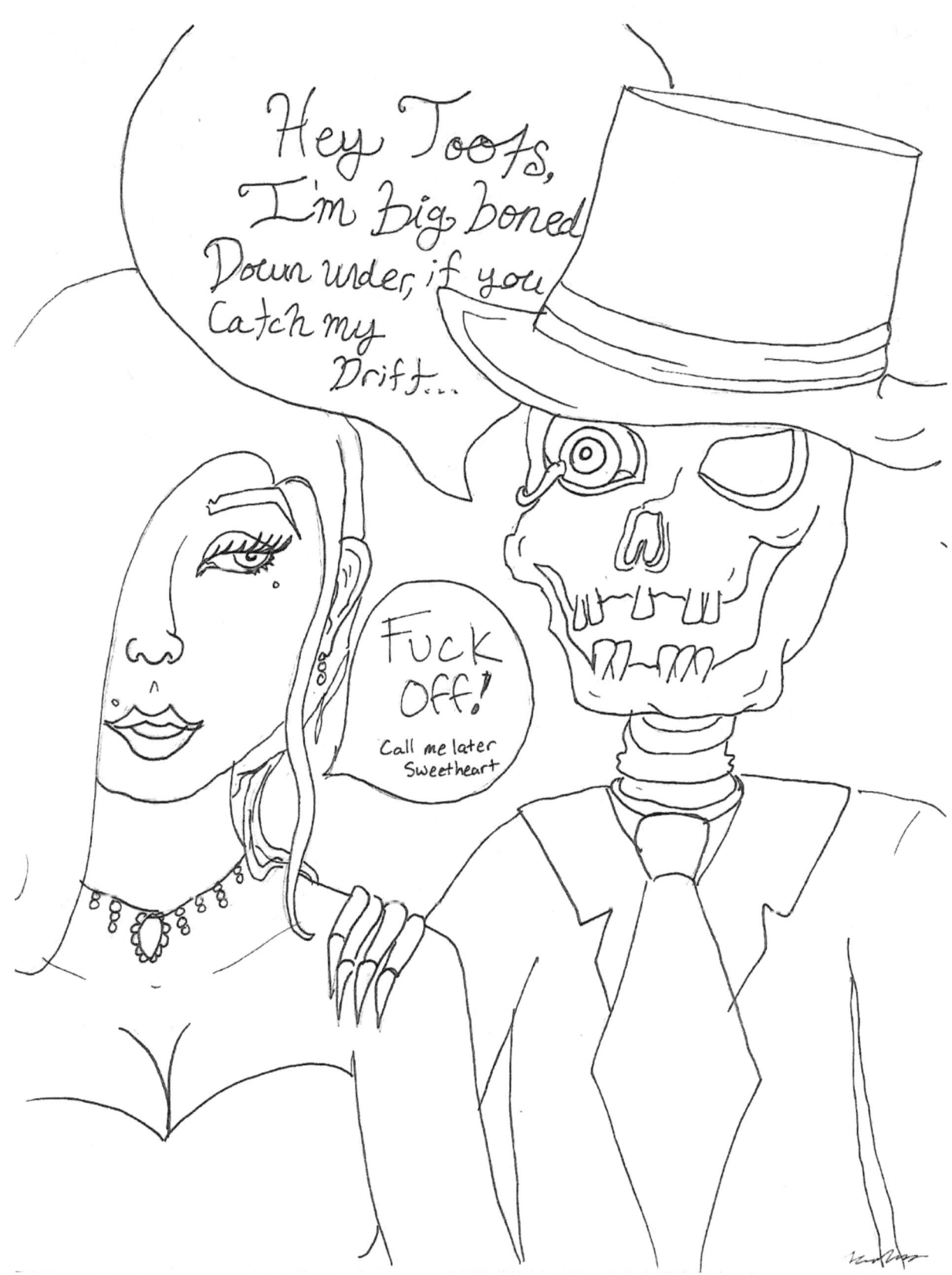

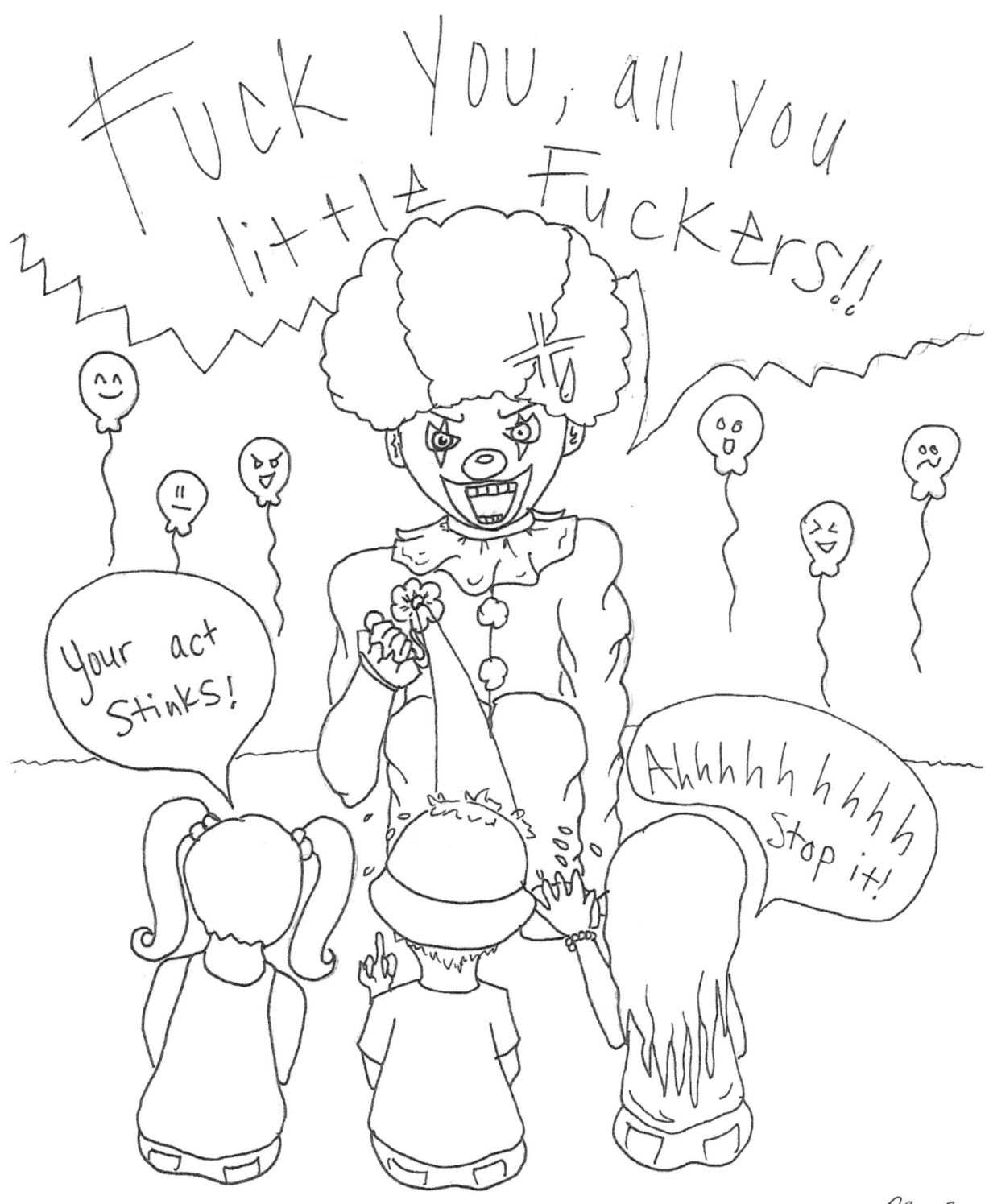

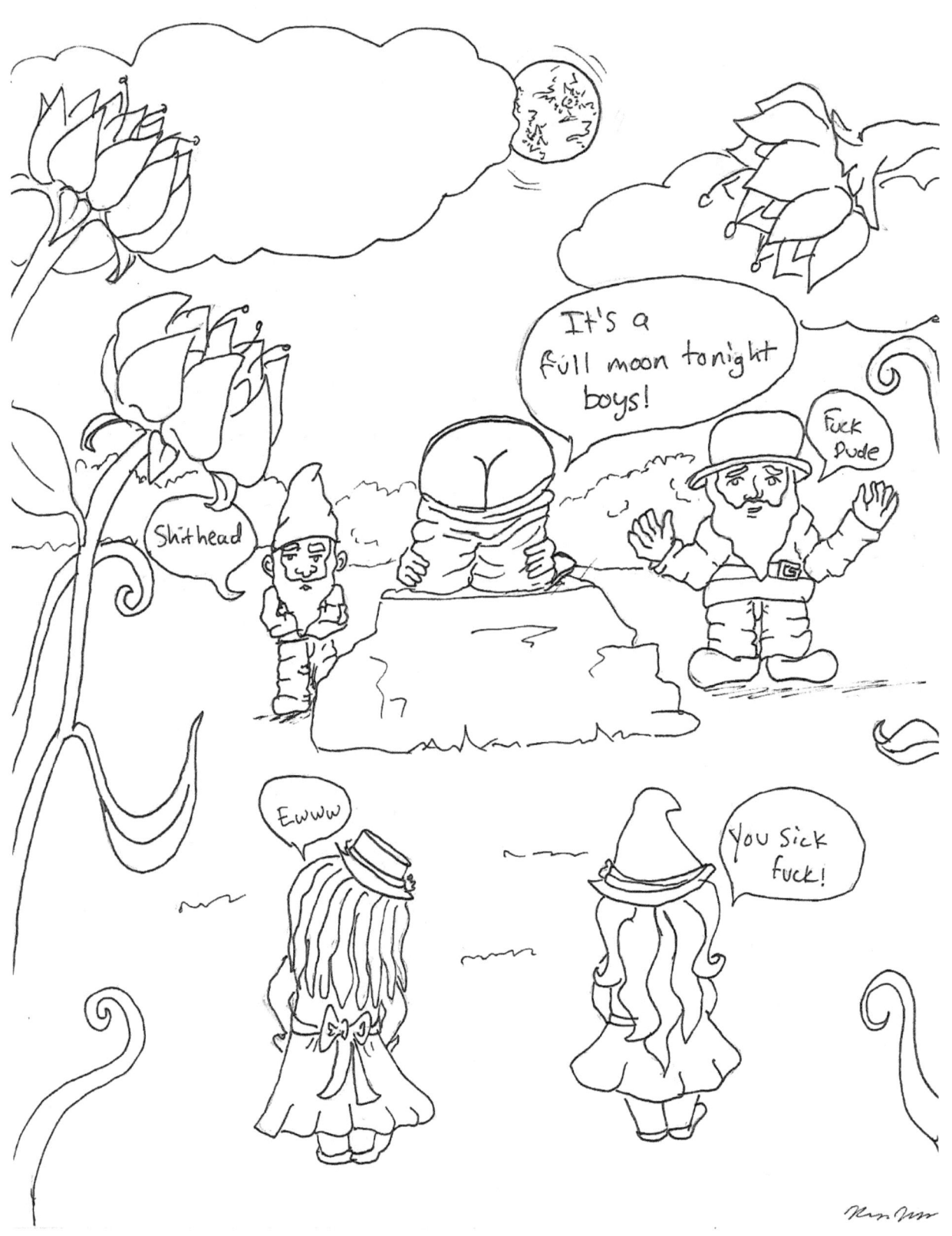

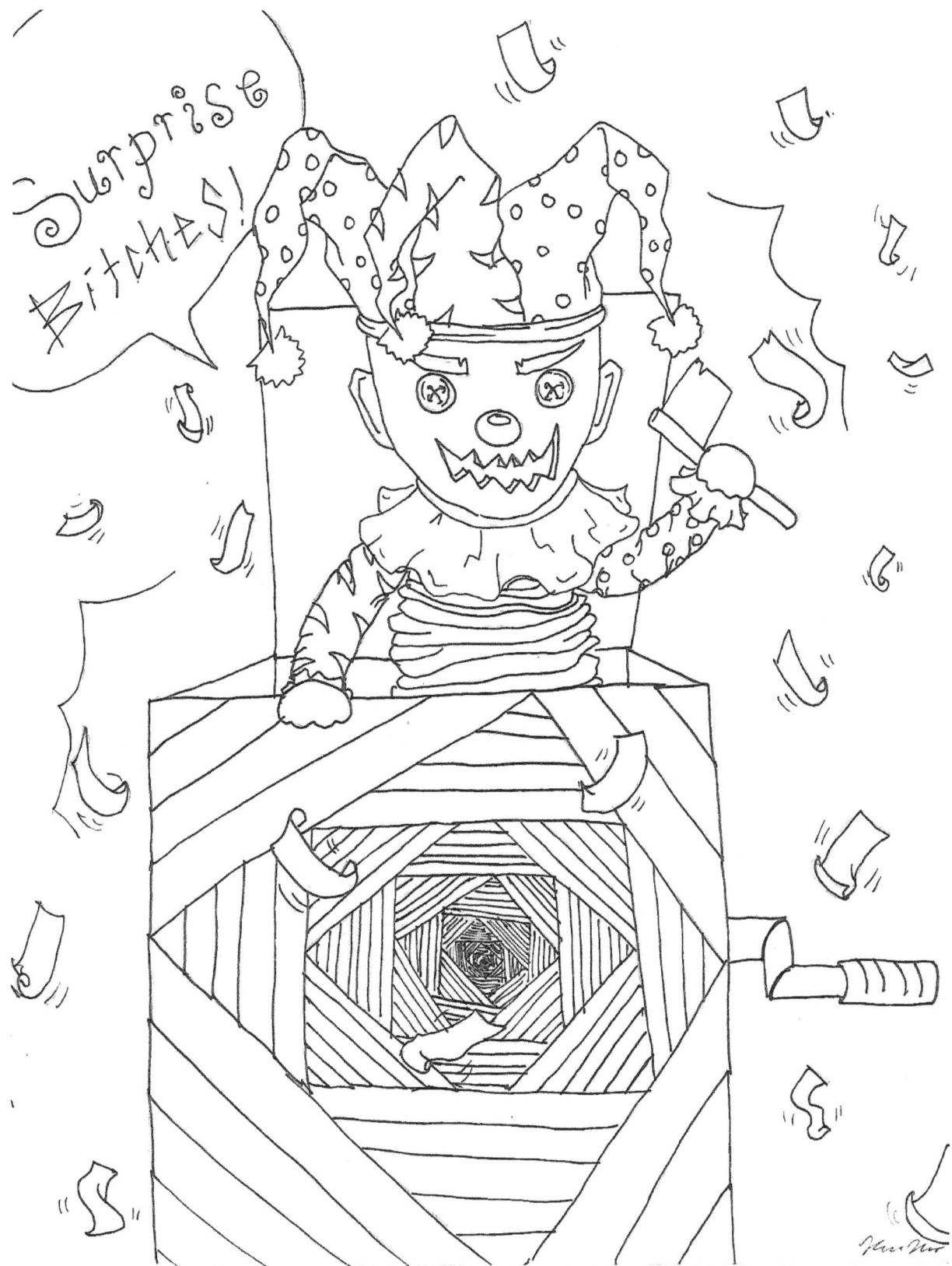

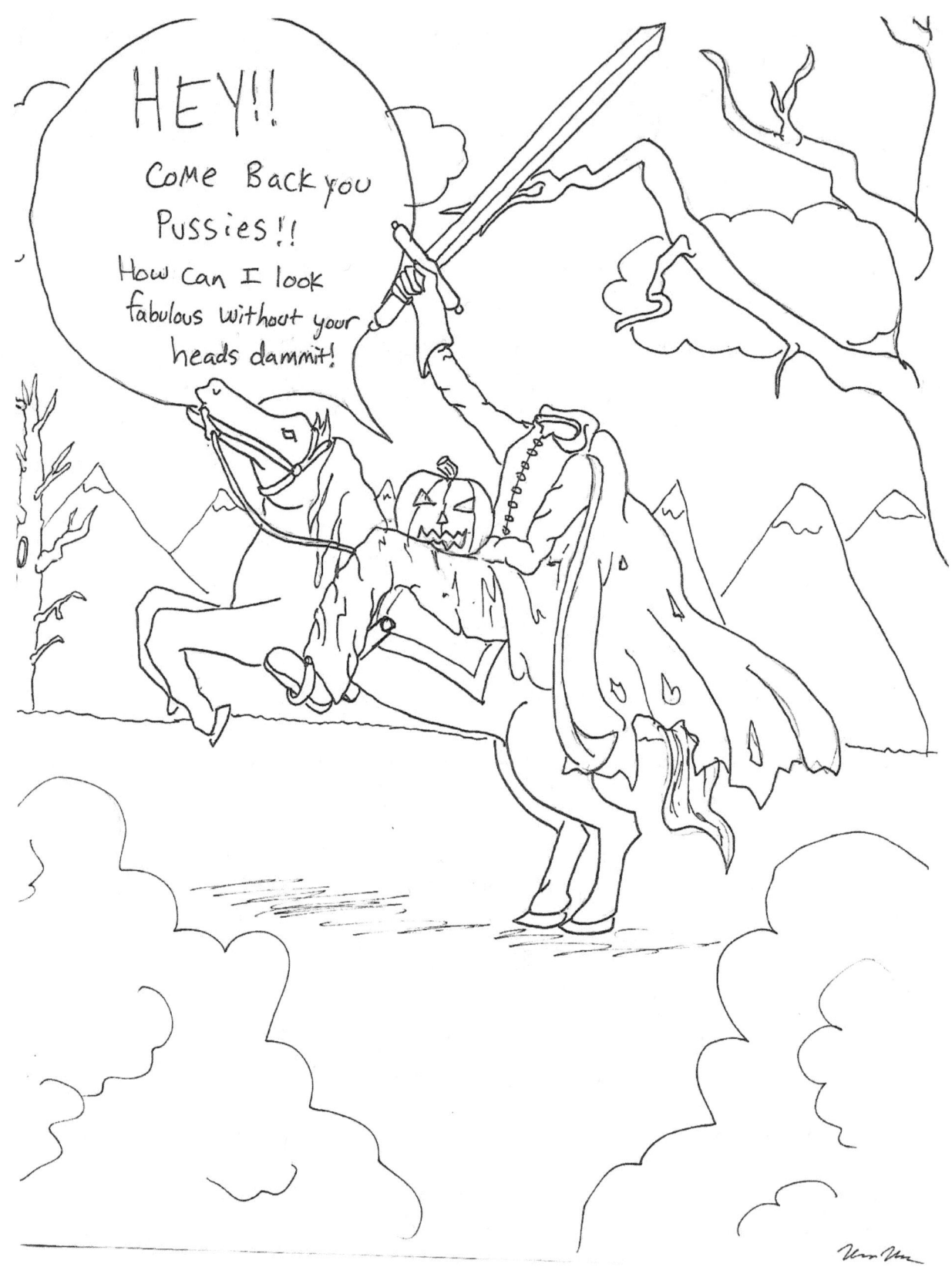

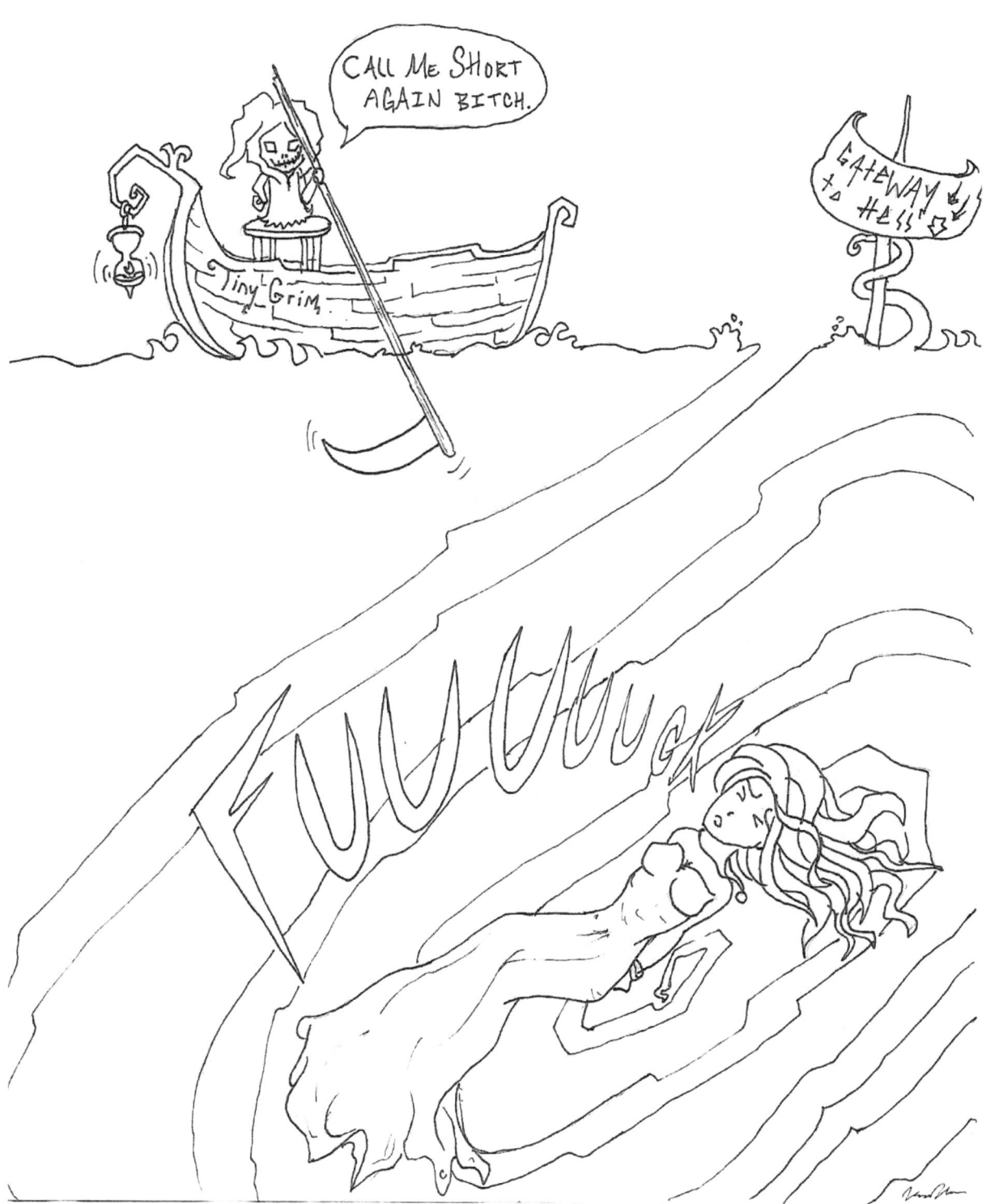

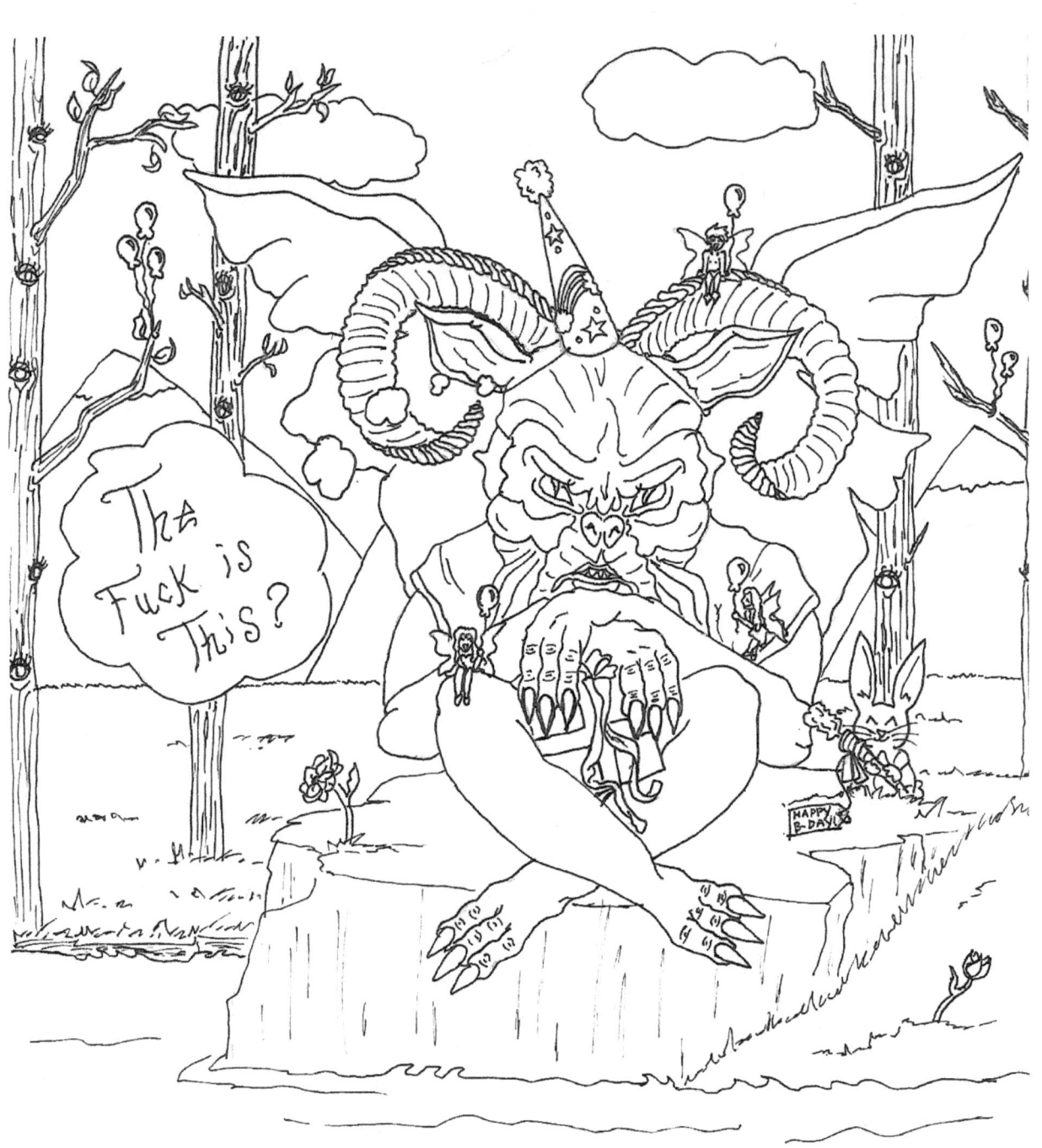

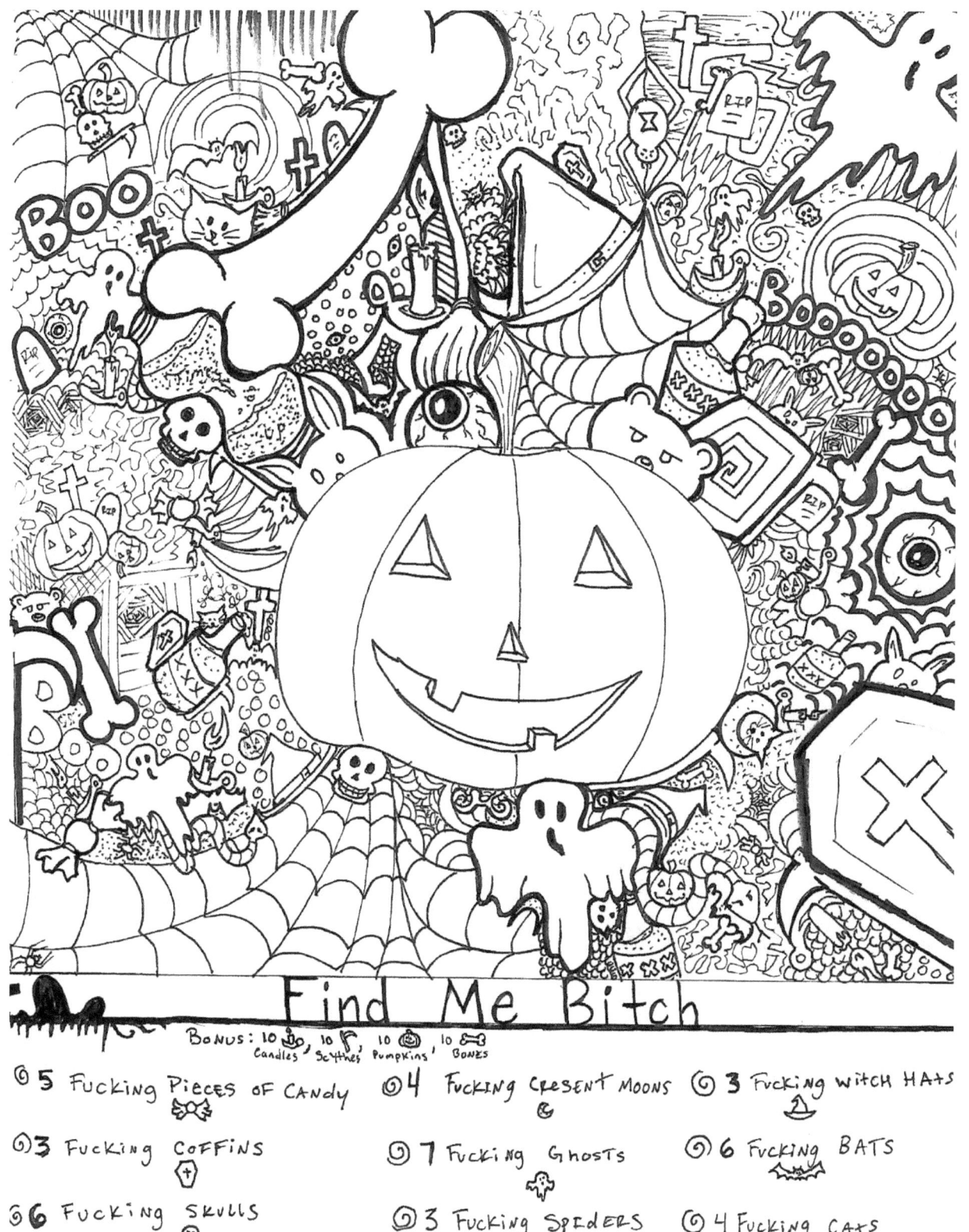

Find Me Bitch

Bonus: 10 Candles, 10 Scythes, 10 Pumpkins, 10 Bones

- 5 Fucking Pieces of Candy
- 4 Fucking Cresent Moons
- 3 Fucking Witch Hats
- 3 Fucking Coffins
- 7 Fucking Ghosts
- 6 Fucking Bats
- 6 Fucking Skulls
- 3 Fucking Spiders
- 4 Fucking Cats